Wild Hogs

& *Peccaries*

Southwestern peccary, also called Javelinas or Razorbacks.

Disruptive Invaders

Dr. Richard A. NeSmith

Love of Nature Series

ISSUE 27

Applied Principles of Education & Learning

APE-Learning

dr.nesmith@gmail.com

https://bit.ly/3ZRFdDs

Dr. Richard A. NeSmith

JUNE 2025

ISBN: 9798586675309

FLESCH-KINCAID GRADE LEVEL: 8.6

Wild Hogs & Peccaries

(Sus *scrofa* and Pecari)

In North America, there are two types of wild or feral swine or hogs. Wild mammals are those species that depend upon themselves to find their own food, water, and shelter. **Peccary**[1] and **wild hogs**[2] are both **ungulates** (hoofed animals). The Peccary[3] is also called *razorback* hog, collared peccaries, Mexico musk hog, or *Javelina* (pronounced, ha-vuh-lee-nuhs).[4]

Overall, people tend to like pigs in general. These animals

have even become popular and given humanlike qualities in fables, cartoons, and Hollywood movies.[5] Most children

---

[1] Pecari is a genus of mammals in the peccary family, Tayassuidae.

[2] And of the Suidae family.Genus/species: Sus *scrofa*

[3] Genus/species: Dicotyles *tajacu*

[4] With the numerous names, we may even refer to them simply as "pigs" or "wild pigs," understanding that we are speaking of wild or feral swine.

[5] Known as anthropomorphism - the attribution of human characteristics or behavior to a god, animal, or object

have heard of the *Three Little Pigs*. And, children of old enjoyed Porky and Petunia Pig. Even today's children have not been left out of the contemporary creation of a loving Peppa Pig cartoon. Movies like

Babe, Gordy, Charlotte's Web, Wilbur, and *My Brother the Pig* have always been popular entertainment.

We will see that these mammals are some of the smartest animals in the forest. They possess some of the most complex and often problematic behaviors that

might explain why they are *among the most* **disruptive** *of all mammals* living in North America.

The wild boar was introduced in the 1500s by Spanish explorer and Conquistador Hernando DeSoto. He brought these across the sea as a food source for a long and unpredictable journey. In essence, the wild boars are feral, having escaped from

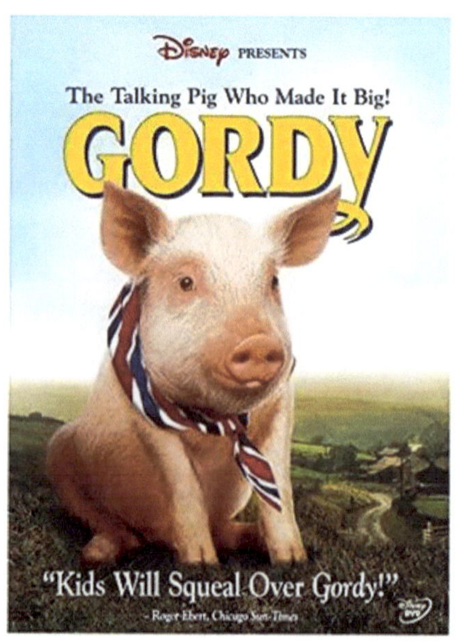

4

Collared peccaries, also called Javelinas, thrive in the greater southwestner US States..

the free-range livestock management practices then and during colonization of the eastern United States. Wild pig populations spread rapidly.

Peccaries are not entirely native (**indigenous**) either, in North America. They are a tropical species, which naturally restricts their range, and may have been introduced as early as the 1700s.

A term frequently used to describe species that have been **introduced** from another ecosystem is the term **invasive species**. At first, the criteria for an invasive species include

1. **It is non-native to the ecosystem under consideration.**

2. **Its introduction is likely to cause economic or environmental harm or harm to human health.**

There are more specific criteria, but at this point, it is

enough to state that invasive species:

❶ **have an advantage over native species due to lack of predators or common diseases,**

❷ **propagate or multiply much more quickly,**

❸ **they create or change the environment in harmful ways.**

Those introduced species that do not create harm are not considered to be invasive. One rule of thumb seems to be that the greater the invasive species population is, the more significant its impact. Hogs have greatly affected, damaging forests, croplands, and water resources, including hosting **diseases** that can threaten humans, wildlife, and livestock.[6] Invasive species often displace native species and may even

dominate the habitat. Feral pigs are in the top 100 invasive species in the world. The estimated annual cost of invasive

---

[6] Wild pigs are capable of carrying and transmitting at least 30 bacterial, fungal, and viral diseases which threaten humans, livestock, and wildlife, some of those which can infect humans are brucellosis, leptospirosis, toxoplasmosis, and trichinosis. Though disease transmission to humans is a real concern, the largest threat from wild pig diseases is the potential transmission to domestic livestock.

plant and animal species in the United States is estimated to be $137 billion.

Not addressed often in the ***invasive v. non-invasive*** debate is: *when* should an invasive species be considered "native"? Our example here is with wild hogs who have lived on this continent for over five hundred years. And though the peccaries have been residents much longer, some still insist they, too, are invasive. Nevertheless, the impact invasive species have on the environment and the ecosystem is always tremendous and changes the very dynamics that occur among living things, and the wild hogs are most definitely doing that. These wild hogs and Javelinas are both considered the most disruptive invasive species in the United States.

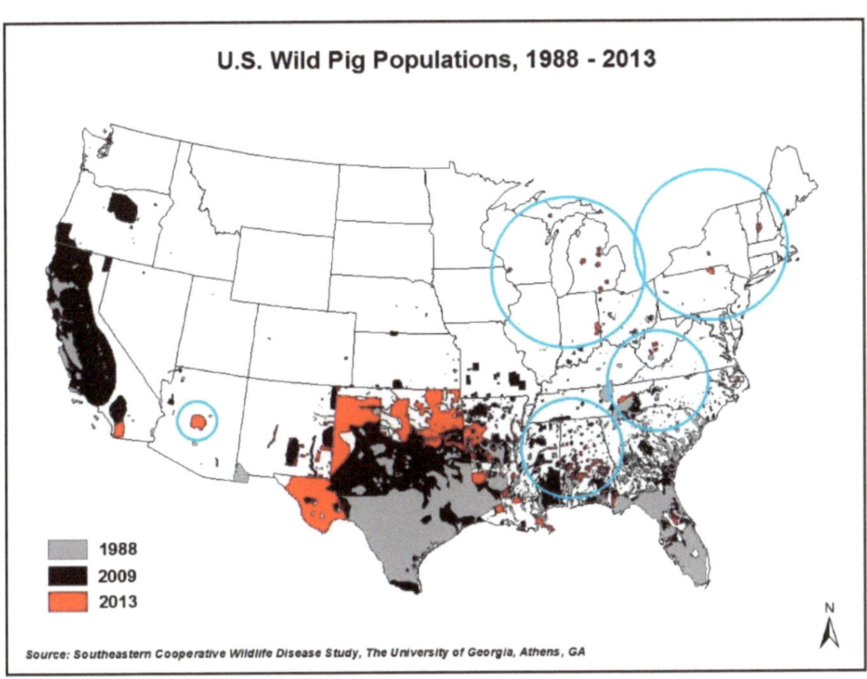

Range

A **boar** is an uncastrated male domestic pig, but it also means a *wild pig of any gender*. A **hog** often means a domestic pig that weighs more than 120 lbs. (54 kilograms) and describes feral or wild boars.

The species is now one of the *widest-ranging* mammals globally and the most widespread of **nonruminant**[7] **mammals**. It is reported now that the population of wild hogs is at 9 million in the U.S. alone. **Their population has expanded from about 18 states to at least 45 over the last three decades.** In the last few years, they have

Rooting involves getting the nose down below the grass line in search for tender root and grubs, larvae, and worms.

---

[7] Animals that ruminate chew their "cud," meaning they have 4 stomachs, of which the first holds the unchewed portion of plant material.

established themselves in Canada[8] and are encroaching on border states like Montana and North Dakota. About 50 percent of the nation's feral pigs live in Texas. Fifty thousand wild boar have left Texas and invaded inside 400 miles (643 km) of the Mexican border. These plague-like levels create problems in four different Mexican States, including the communities around Ojinaga and Coyame de Sotol.

The **peccaries**, or **Javelinas**,[9] are found in the southwest United States, specifically in Arizona, Texas, and New Mexico, where they live in desert habitats. The Javelina (Peccary) population is estimated to be 250,000 in the U.S. The Texas population is nearly 200,000, with another 45,000 in Arizona and 5,000 in New Mexico (see map

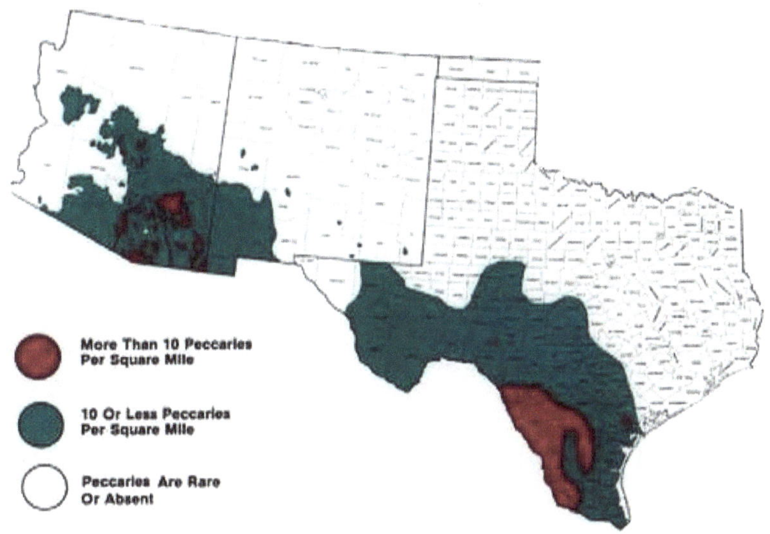

below). The peccaries' range is limited by cold temperature.

---

[8] In the 1980s and 1990s, the Eurasian boar first arrived in Canada, imported as livestock or for hunting. They escaped or were released, and sometimes mated with domestic pigs. Their descendants have now become common across the Canadian prairie.

[9] The spearlike canine teeth give the peccary its common names javelin and javelina.

They lack underfur and appear to be unable to withstand harsh winters as a result.

We see that those closest to 1 (red color) have the greatest increase in the wild pig population from the map below.[10]

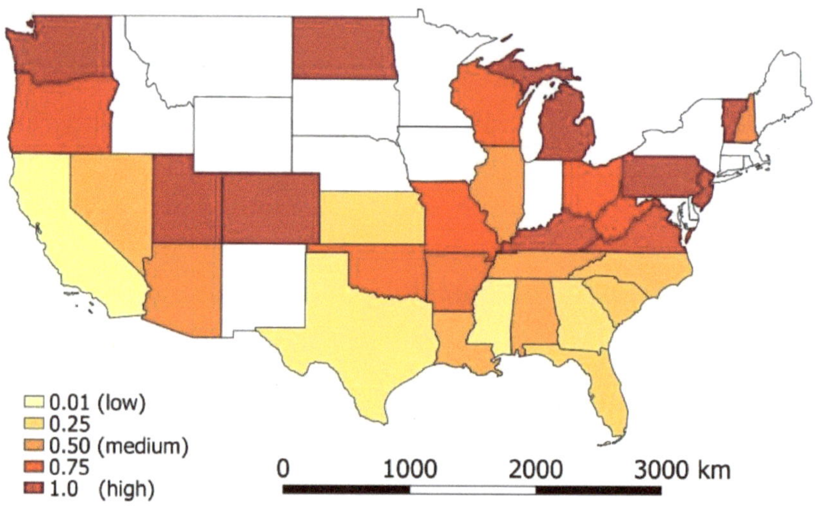

Values closer to 1 indicate newly invaded states and states that have experienced relatively high population growth and range expansion since 2004. States not included in these analyses are depicted by white.

INTRODUCTION TO MAMMALS

Mammals number nearly 500 species in North America. To better understand these hogs, we need to consider what a mammal is and its characteristics. There are *five traits that all mammals share*: These include that they are:

1. covered with hair or fur

2. warm-blooded

---

[10] Note that for the states not shown, IN, NE, and NM exhibited reduced population size from 2016 compared to 2004 due to eradication efforts and CT, DE, ID, IA, ME, MD, MA, MN, MT, NY, RI, SD, and WY exhibited zero wild pigs in 2004 and 2016. See United States Department of Agriculture report available at: https://www.aphis.usda.gov/wildlife_damage/nwrc/publications/19pubs/rep2019-050.pdf

3. usually born alive and relatively well-developed

4. fed while very young with milk after birth produced by mammary glands

5. larger and more complex brains than any other group of animals

Warm-blooded animals are considered **endothermic**, meaning they create the needed body heat from food and energy breakdown (**metabolism**), typically generated by the liver. This means that a mammal's **body temperature** is maintained at a near-constant level regardless of the external conditions.

Mammals also carry their unborn in the **uterus**[11] for more extended periods of time than other animals, which is called **gestation**.[12] This time spent developing in the uterus

---

[11] Uterus is the organ in a female mammal in which the young develop prior to birth.
[12] Gestation is the length of time a mammal develops and grows inside its mother's body before being born.

varies in length from 13 days (as in the opossum) to 210

days (as in the whitetail deer).[13] Of course, a manatee's gestation is 11 months, but elephants' have the most prolonged gestation, approaching 22 months.

Characteristics

The wild boars and peccaries are more similar than different. The wild boar is bulky, stocky, and heavy in size with short and relatively thin legs. They can reach 3 to 6.5 feet (0.9-1.98 m) in length, 21.6 to 39.3 inches (54.86-98.3 cm) in height, and 90 to 700 pounds (40.8-317.5 kg) in weight.

The body of wild boars is covered with a double coat of fur that can be brown, red, black, or grey. The neck nearly does not exist, so the head appears to run into a bulge, making almost a bump appearance behind the shoulder blades, leading to a short and full-bodied trunk. Therefore, the

<hr>

[13] See *Love of Nature series*, Issues: 13 (Opossums: Misunderstood Critter), and 25 (Deer: Nature's Timid but Elegant).

swine does not appear to be able to move the neck but instead sways its body left or right in place of turning its huge head, which makes up one-third of its body. The hindquarters almost seem too small to match the front.

Closely resembling the wild pig, the peccaries have dark

Up to three layers of bristlly, coarse hair during the winter coat.

long, coarse, and bristly hair (giving it a shaggy appearance) and a large head with a round snout. These hair layer lengths change with the seasons, being longer in winter and shorter in summer. The ears are smaller, as is the tail, which is generally not visible. There are skeletal and dental differences. The Javelin's teeth do not protrude but make notable lumps in the lips.

The head is somewhat of a conical shape, starting with a narrow snout well suited for digging. With the head down, the bill digs into the ground like a plow turning up the soil and roots several inches deep. With strong neck muscles, the swine can push its nose upward, upturning a great deal

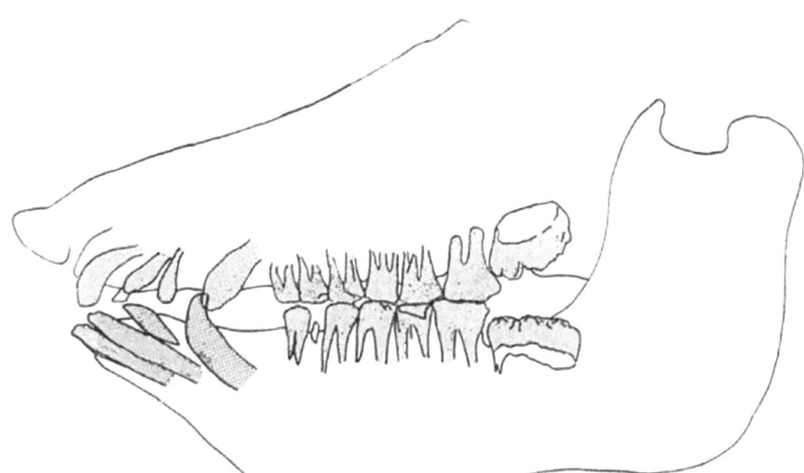

Front incisors of wild hogs are very close together. The front incisors of domesticated hogs, however, are spread far apart with gaps.

of soil and sod 3-4 inches (8-10 cm deep). This nose digging and plowing is referred to as **rooting** (from the old English meaning "to turn up ground" or "to dig."

These swine have small, deep-set eyes and long and wide ears. The ears are a bit unseemly and flop as they walk. During the mid-1500s, they used an old saying that stated, "You can't make a silk purse out of a sow's ear, meaning one is *unable to turn something ugly or inferior into something attractive or of value.*

They have well-developed canine teeth that jut from the mouth of adult males. Each side has opposing canines that grind up against the other, providing a "self-sharpening" effect, especially on the lower canine teeth (**tusks**).[14]

---

[14] Also called *tushes.*

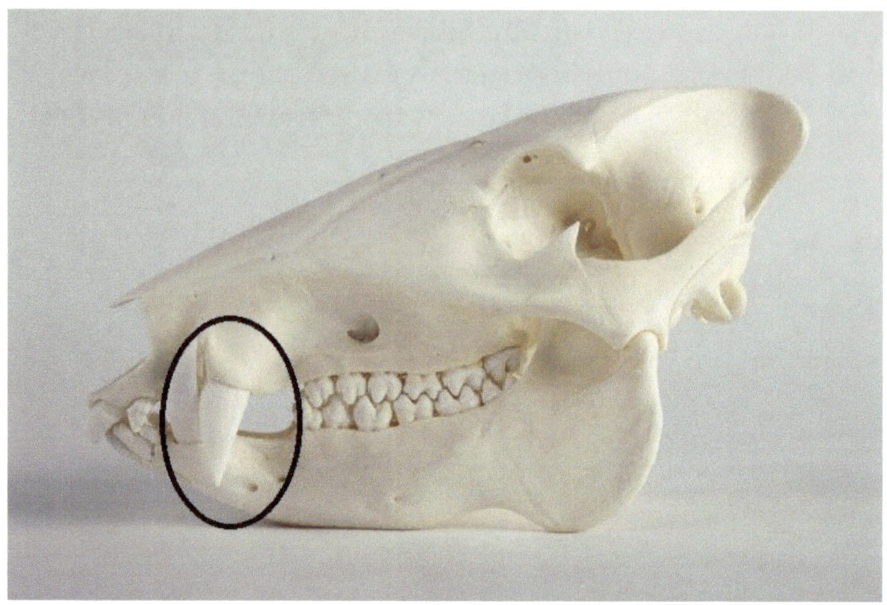

Canine teeth on upper and lower jaws forms tusk. The upper ones sharpen the lower ones to make these razor sharp.

Enamel covers the forward-facing sides of the tooth, while the rear-facing surface is covered by cementum.[15]

Those upper teeth are known as whetters (as in whetstones), which sharpen the lower curved teeth called *cutters*. These tusks erupt at about 7 to 13 months of age.

In both males (**boars**) and females (gilts or **sows**)[16], the upper tusks usually are shorter than the lower ones. The tusks, though in both sexes, are more prominent in males and are sharper and longer. The upper tusks of sows tend to extend downward, whereas in an upper direction for the

---

[15] Cementum a specialized calcified substance covering the root of a tooth. Its purpose is the anchor or support the tooth to the bone.

[16] The distinction is that gilts are female hogs who have never given birth, whereas, sows have produced offspring.

boars.[17]

Tusks grow at a rate of about one-fourth inch per month. However, most of this growth is lost through grinding wear against the upper tusk. And, like that of rodents, the lower teeth of hogs continue to grow, and inadequate grinding can cause them to grow upward into the hog's mouth and the jaw (**mandible**). This issue is rarely seen in *wild* swine.

As **quadrupeds** (four-legged), the feet are made of **hooves**, with an almost C-shaped (semi-circular) lateral footprint. These harden upon maturity but remain capable of rapid movements. Wild hogs can run at a maximum speed of 25 miles per hour (40 kph), though an average rate is closer to 11 mph (17.3 kph). Also, they have been

Male with a growing mane down the upper back.

observed to jump 4.5 to 5 feet (1.4-1.5 m). The ability to move so quickly and with such sharp tusks can make these hazardous animals. Though possibly useful for digging, the tusks are truly for defense and are razor-sharp. Combine the razored teeth with the extra strong neck muscles, and this animal can *slice* and *dice*!

The presence of **sexual dimorphism** is also demonstrated. The boars are generally 5-10 percent larger and 20-30%

---

[17] These differences are so characteristic that these teeth can be used to accurately determine the sex of feral hogs that are over 14 months of age. Teeth are also used to determine age. See: https://www.aphis.usda.gov/wildlife_damage/feral_swine/pdfs/tech-note-aging-feral-swine.pdf

heavier than females. Often the male grows a mane running down the back dorsal, especially during the fall and winter seasons. The peccaries tend to have less sexual differences in appearance and are nearly indistinguishable.

Also, the Peccary's tails are not visible, and their ears are small. Wild hogs have long, hairy tails and large, upright ears. Peccaries have 38 teeth, and pigs have 44 when mature. The hind feet are also different, with peccaries having three toes and pigs having four. Peccaries also have a scent gland on their backs, above their tails, which they use to mark their territory and identify other group members. Males also sport a roughly egg-sized sack near the opening of the penis, which collects urine and emits a sharp foul odor. The function of this sack is not fully understood.

Diet

Wild hogs and peccaries are opportunistic **omnivores**. They have a very diverse diet. They mostly eat vegetable materials, including roots, seeds, fruits, and other animals found in the soil (invertebrates). The fact that they can live on such a variety gives them a significant advantage over most competitors. They eat almost anything (including human bones). This versatile diet increases their survival rate and, thus their population growth.

Though their eyesight and hearing are not their greatest strength, they can see figures 100 yards away and hear a whisper at that same distance. Wild hogs and Javelinas rely more heavily on their sense of smell to find and identify food and warn them of danger. They can sense some odors 5-7 miles (8.0-11.3 km) away and may be able to detect odors as much as 25 feet underground! Also, swine can smell food with their noses underwater or burrow in soil. Though they can, and will, eat meat, they spend most of their time foraging for roots, fungi, and plant matter.

Barrel cactus seem to be a favored food enjoyed by Javelinas.

The digestive tracts of an omnivore are relatively inefficient in digesting plant fiber. Scientists have just recently pinpointed the locations within the digestive tract of hogs

where the fiber is fermented.[18]

Wild hogs and peccaries favor fruits, grains, and seeds. With their terrific sense of smell, pigs are attracted to fruits and vegetables, especially overripe ones. They are well adapted for **_rooting_** up roots, bulbs, tubers, and rhizomes. They sometimes munch on grasses and leaves and complement this plant-based diet with fungi, worms, grubs, insects, eggs, snakes, other young animals, and scavenge for carrion (remains of already-dead or decaying animals). In addition to the normal foraging diet, the Javelina will often feed for days on any overturned _barrel cactus_. They start eating at the root and will tunnel completely into the cactus. Cactus seems to be food these swine enjoy eating.

---

[18] The site of fermentation for soluble fiber was either in the small intestine or in the cecum, where insoluble fiber fermentation occurrs in the colon.

Wild boars have numerous social groupings, the basic being the sow and her piglets.

Those living in the southwestern states sometimes have trouble keeping the Javelinas out of their yards and gardens.

Habitats

A group of peccaries traveling and living together is called a **squadron**. A group of hogs is called a **passel** or **team, sounder** or **herd**, with small or unique distinctions in each. For example, a **sounder** is a herd of feral hogs making up a distinctive social group, primarily comprised of one or more adult sows and one or multiple generations of offspring (**piglets**). One or more mature boars will spend time with a sounder when trying to mate with a sow but then move on, searching for another sow.

Unlike most wild boars, peccaries live in *dry arid habitats.* Feral hogs, however, show a preference for river banks (**riparian**) and wetland habitats. Swine are good swimmers, and some even seem to enjoy swimming. Also, wild boars willingly adjust to habitat changes caused by fire, logging, and natural disasters, except those that result in a loss in production of the fruit of forest trees and shrubs, such as **acorns** and other **nuts** (called **mast**). Extreme flooding and heavy snowfall will cause wild hogs to move on to more suitable environments.

Feral hogs occupy and exploit a wide variety of habitats. Wild hogs need four resources on a year-round basis to survive. These include:

❶ **a reliable and seasonally-available food source**

❷ **daily access to well-distributed water**

❸ **shade**

❹ **escape cover**

But as far as ecosystems, wild boars can thrive in various

Many watering holes become contaminated after wild hogs use it frequently.

environments, including plains, mountains,[19] humid swamps, and dry uplands. They generally prefer remote areas and avoid densely populated areas close to human

civilization. They inhabit elevations from sea level up to 13,000 ft above mean sea level. However, these animals do not tend to high mountain areas with substantial winter snowfall or intensive agricultural areas where cover is scarce.

Behavior

Wild hogs and Javelinas may have some of the most complex and varied behaviors than any mammal in North America. Feral hogs are, in fact, unique in many ways among the native and introduced game. The degree of land and property **destruction** has caused a great deal of observation and research to be conducted on these **ungulates** by those

---

[19] They adhere to and generally obeys Bergmann's rule, which states that while larger subspecies are found towards higher latitude smaller subspecies live at lower attitude.

responsible for conserving land resources.

Intelligence and Complex Behavior

Land management practices and strategies for other wildlife mammals do not seem to work with feral hogs. Hogs are very intelligent and elusive and are believed to be among the most intelligent animals on the planet, following chimps, dolphins, and elephants. Overall, research has shown that pigs are skilled at mazes and other tests requiring object location and have excellent long-term memories. They can even use a mirror to find hidden food.

Stalking wild swine is very different from actually seeing them in the wild. The mess left behind is very telltale signs, such as rooting, trampling, **wallows**, and tree or post rubs. They are messy eaters and have messy habits. They often destroy established plants uprooting and turning soil. They cause damage to agricultural fields, crops, forests, streams, and the general

environment in which they live. Possibly most important, they can impair the regeneration of plants, grass, shrubs, and trees through consumption and destruction of seedlings,[20] particularly those of longleaf pines. Because of this destruction, they require territories of 450–750 acres (but may range wider in search of food during poorer growing seasons or conditions).

During the cooler months of the year, hogs may be active and feed during day and night. However, if hunting pressure or temperatures are high, they will seek cover during the day, and feed and be most active at night.

Social and Organized

Swine are **social** animals. The basic social unit is the sow and her litter and is a ***matriarchal society***. Male swine tend to be mostly **solitary**. However, peccary males live in a hierarchical grouping, with a dominant male leading the

---

[20] Researchers suspected that pigs chew the roots of seedlings, swallow the sap and starches, and then spit out the woody tissue. To support this idea, researchers have found and documented balls of masticate roots where wild pigs have been rooting among woody plants. For more information, see: https://www.aphis.usda.gov/wildlife_damage/feral_swine/pdfs/managing-feral-pigs.pdf

herd. Larger groups (called **sounders**) often develop with two to six females and their offspring. To say that these groups can become complicated is an understatement, for such can be categorized into eleven groupings:

1. single adults
2. adult groups
3. single subadults
4. subadult groups
5. groups of both adults and subadults
6. basic family groups (*one adult with piglets*)
7. sounders (*several adults with piglets*)
8. extended family groups (*adults with both piglets and subadults*)
9. single piglets
10. piglet groups
11. subadult and piglets groups

Depending upon a wild hog's gender and age, an individual

may temporarily occupy any one of eleven groupings. Group sizes vary significantly with populations from 2 to 30 or more. Sounders organize around two or three closely related females who are reproductively mature. These can contain two or three related females and their litters. There are times when the abundance of resources, including food, watering holes (in arid areas), or dry spells, brings together over one hundred individuals for short periods. These massive groupings are localized spectacles and disperse rather quickly.

These feral hogs live complicated social lives and learn from one another while working and foraging together.

They can distinguish between familiar pigs and strangers. Like canine puppies, they also play and play-fight. Their domesticated relatives have even been shown to show compassion or empathy. And their domesticated cousins could also rather accurately sense or predict whether a person would be nice to them or not.[21]

The tusks are also used in **scent marking**, assisted by a tusk **gland**. Wild hogs and Javelinas are aggressive by nature yet will usually leave humans alone unless feeling threatened. Javelina emits a pungent **odor**, especially if they become alarmed, so one will probably smell them before they see one.

Because feral hogs are very intelligent, secretive, and adaptable, they can exploit a wide variety of geographic locations, habitats, and forage resources. Researchers

---

[21] This trait has also been observed in squirrels. See *Love of Nature* series, Issue 7: Squirrels: Bushy-Ttail Scampers!

observe that wild hogs are more challenging to study than other hoofed animals because of their "intelligence, shyness, and vigilance combined with an acute sense of smell and hearing."

Not only are swine intelligent, but they are relatively clean and hygienic animals. Their sleeping bed is kept separate from their latrine areas. Most people believe that pigs are messy and relate more to how they are kept on farms and roll around in the mud to cool off. Hogs do have a few sweat glands, but they are inefficient in cooling down their bodies.

Clean but Pragmatic

Wild hogs and Peccaries are not known for grooming. However, it would be incorrect to think that grooming is not essential or not done. It is, but a **symbiotic relationship**[22] is at play in which various species of birds physically forage off of the feral hogs for external parasites. The Florida scrub jays, crows, and black-billed magpies are all known to groom wild hogs. Whether standing, walking, or lying down, feral hogs are visited by these birds that often ride or stand on their backs. Whether immature or mature, the hogs will solicit these birds by

---

[22] A close and long-term biological relationship between two different biological organisms, be it mutualistic, commensalistic, or parasitic. In this case, the bird would benefit by obtaining food (such as ticks) while hogs benefit by having those parasites removed.

approaching them and waiting for grooming to begin.

Habits

Like most mammals, hogs are creatures of habit and establish routines. A wild hog's daily activity, however, varies by location and region. The factors already mentioned influence behaviors and routines, and proximity to humans also plays a factor. Wild hogs are never always **diurnal** (active during daylight hours) or **nocturnal** (active during night hours). In isolated or undisturbed habitats, wild hogs tend to be more diurnal. In areas where hunting pressure or human activity exists, wild hogs tend to be more nocturnal. In Javelinas, they tend to be diurnal in the winter and nocturnal during winter.

Activity patterns can also be seasonally driven. Such can be seen with wild hogs being more active during the nights in the summer months because of the daytime heat. And more **crepuscular** (twilight hours) during the spring and fall.

Daily activity patterns also vary between the males and the

females. Sows maintain more constant activity for more extended periods. In contrast, the males display brief bursts

Establishing a dominant hierarchy begins immediately at birth, and piglets challenge for the best place to suckle. The teats closer to the head deliver more milk. Runts often do not survive. Pigs are completely weaned by about 3 months of age.

of movement followed by lengthy times of relative inactivity.

The general movement of most wild hogs is characteristic of just plain general wandering or drifting. This wandering, granted, is restricted to their **home range**. This routine relates closely to the typical search for food, population density, quality of the habitat, reproduction activities, season, climate conditions and temperature, their social interactions, and, of course, disturbance by humans. A change in any of these causes a change in routine. For example, should food supply become limited, then more searching and wandering occurs or alternative forage resources are sought.

Hogs like to rest or nap, so beds can be unique for the purpose, including the creation of loafing or resting beds.

These structures are similar to but less complex than the **farrowing** (time when giving birth to piglets) nests. Loafing or resting beds can be used more than once, with some individuals returning to use a specific bed repeatedly. Some beds are very simple depressions in the ground, whereas others can be quite elaborate. Wild hogs typically seek out thick underbrush for security or root into a brush pile or downed treetops for protection. They can simply lie down and sleep, usually on their sides. In the hot months, they will often lay in the mud or seek deep shade. And, they like to *snuggle* and will sleep nose to nose.

Home Range

A home range is established by each group and by each male hog. This is an area in which they *live* and restrict their movements. It is a defined area over an extended period. As long as the home range provides for their needs, they remain. Home ranges average six square miles (15.6 km²). The home range size is determined by several factors already mentioned and the animals' body weight and the local hog population density. Areas that do not meet these needs will cause the home range to increase in size, which often occurs seasonally.

Boars have more extensive home ranges than sows Sows will reduce their home range just before giving birth and when their litters are being nursed. Boars are, generally, more mobile daily than sows. Intensive hunting, shooting, or dog yapping will cause wild boars to move to more remote places several miles away permanently.

Locomotion

Movement and mobility in feral hogs follow the standard **gaits** or steps (patterns of footfalls; see illustration below) seen in other large hoofed mammals. This includes walking, trotting, galloping, and running. Besides, the faster non-walking gaits visually have a "bouncing" trot, a "rocking" sprint, and a "steady/flat" flex-extension gallop or run. Feral hogs typically travel at a rate of 1-3 miles per hour. These animals are sure-footed, rapid runners and can travel relatively fast over open ground, reaching speeds of up to 20-30 miles per hour.

In addition to being quick-footed on the ground, larger feral hogs can

Javelina

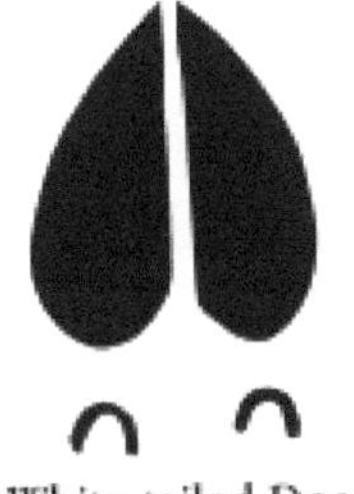

White-tailed Deer

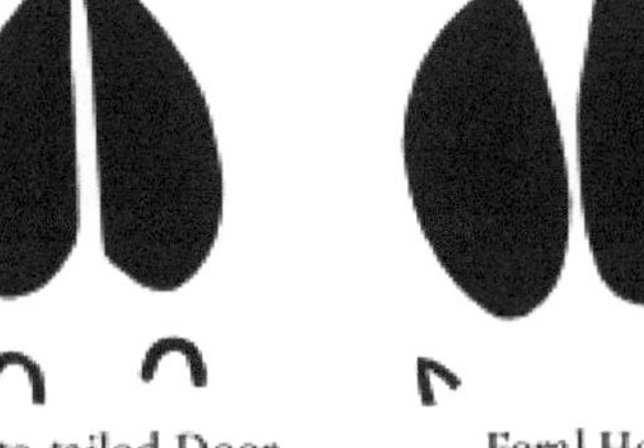

Feral Hog

also physically jump over barriers as high as 3 feet. They can cross average to large-sized rivers and channels and open waters up to 4 miles across, being strong swimmers.

Protective and Aggressive

Wild boars and Javelinas can be very aggressive, especially is this so amongst females toward one another. As they mature, aggression increases, as does

A comparison of different body shapes of the wild boars and Javelinas. Wild boars are much larger in size.

their weight.[23] The same aggression is noted with males but is usually restricted to establishing hierarchy and dominance, establishing breeding rights rather than foraging rights as seen in females.[24] Fighting can become intense, resulting in injury or even death.

We often consider humans to be emotionally complex and sometimes hang our feelings on our sleeves. "Wild hogs

---

[23] The weight in maturing male feral hogs increases until 3 years of age due to testicular hormones, and then decreases after 5 years of age. The body mass of mature boars has been reported to drop during the breeding season, with some individuals losing up to 20-25% of their body weight. This is due to a combination of increased testosterone production and the resulting reduced foraging done by these boars at that time.

[24] A European and Russian wild boar were introduced in the early 1900s into the United States for hunting. Today's wild boars are often mixed with these foreign breeds. For more information see: https://www.wildpiginfo.msstate.edu/about/history.php

display their moods through physical cues. Their physical posture or body language can generally determine an individual feral hog's mood or momentary temperament at any particular time. The different ***mannerisms*** and postures described for these animals include:

❶ an aggressive stance,

❷ a threatening charge,

❸ a submissive posture,

❹ a curiosity or alert posture, and

❺ play among juvenile animals.

As a group, feral hogs have a team approach to scanning and warning of trespassing or intruding predators. The larger the group, the more surveillance and detection, but the less from each individual. It would be like instead of 5 pigs sharing 20% of their attention on detection; ten pigs might only attribute 10% towards monitoring such. The

scanning done by individual animals decreases with the increase of the group size. This behavior was also markedly different between solitary hogs and groups of any size. The solitary animals did significantly more visual scanning.

Communication

Wild hogs also communicate in rather sophisticated ways. More than 20 different vocalizations have been identified. These include loud woofs, grunts, squeals, roars, and growls. Even general grunts have various tones; low grunts, nursing grunts, feeding grunts, and teeth-clacking or popping sounds. **Piglets** and female hogs typically are more vocal than mature males.

The enigma of pigs being clean creatures and yet **wallowing** in nasty mud is ever-present. Wallowing is rolling about or relaxing in the mud. However, this behavior becomes clearer as one realizes that wallowing serves three specific functions. First, with few efficient

Problems often occur when wildlife become accustomed to people (habituation). Wild hogs naturally seek to avoid humans.

sweat glands,[25] pigs wallow in mud *to cool off* their body temperature through evaporation, which is what sweating does. Secondly, coating the skin with mud acts *to protect the skin* against insects. Though a year-round practice, wallowing is especially frequent during the summer

---

[25] Feral hogs have and use a number of types of scent glands, including metacarpal glands (back part of the front feet), preorbital glands (nearly bare skin extending from the corner of each eye, preputial glands (located in the folds of skin front of the genitals), and tusk glands (saliva/sebaceous gland). Feral hogs also have proctodaeal glands, perineal glands, mandibular or mental glands, and rhinarium glands. All of these secrete or produce odorous compounds, which may or may not function in scent marking.

months. Wild hogs have been observed during the winter, breaking ice used for wallowing. There is a third possible function, that of marking territory among males during peak breeding season.

Wallowing and Tree Rubs

Wallowing often contaminates water holes and can negatively alter stream habitats. Wallowing and rooting activities are usually found together. Wallowing affects ponds by muddying the waters, spreading diseases, creating algae blooms, bank erosion, destroying aquatic vegetation, and decreasing livestock use and fish production.

As wild boars frequently wallow, **mud rubs** on trees are a good indicator of wild pigs' presence. This behavioral practice provides comfort, removes excess mud, removes hair, and mechanically frees the body of external parasites (hog lice and ticks). Mud rubs on trees can provide an idea of the relative size of pigs in the area. Mud rubs that are 3 to 4 feet off the ground indicate the presence of mature pigs.

Rubs can involve almost any upright sturdy object, including trees (both pines and hardwoods), telephone poles, fences and signposts, rocks and boulders, walls, buildings, and parked cars. In most cases, there is an association between rubs and mud wallows. If a wallow exists, rubs will also be present in the immediate vicinity.

Of the five primary senses, feral hogs tend to use four of these the most: smell, sight, hearing, and touch. Of these, wild hogs excel at the sense of smell. Few other animals have as well evolved and refined a sense of smell as do swine. Feral hogs have good but not great eyesight, and hearing seems to be the least developed of their senses. The sense of touch is centered around the mouth, which they use to touch or pick up and feel objects. Curious or fact-finding bites or chewing are not uncommon when hogs are presented with unknown objects.

Reproduction

Wild hogs breed once or twice per year under favorable conditions.[26] Javelinas breed in the first quarter of the year. Compared to other large mammals, wild hogs have a relatively short gestation period of about 114 days. Sows are sexually mature at 6-8 months of age and average 5-9 piglets per litter. The average sow has up to twelve

---

[26] In most mammals, and some other animals, health and food availability is an important and often a deciding factor on when and how often the breeding season occurs.

mammary glands (**teats**), but all of these may not provide milk (**lactating**). The most generous milk flow is in the teats nearest the head, and the least are towards the back. It is not uncommon or unnatural to see the **runt**[27] of the litter trying to survive on one of the back teats. Boars reach maturity around six months of age but highly dependent on nutrition. Most mature by the 7th or 8th month of age.

Breeding seasons vary. The female can breed during any month, so both sows and boars are capable of breeding year-round. However, as males develop and mature, they are exposed to female **pheromones**[28] , indicating **estrus** (a time when a female is fertile, in heat, or sexually receptive).

---

[27] In a group of animals, a runt is a member that is significantly smaller or weaker than the others. Due to its small size, a runt in a litter faces obvious disadvantages and hardships, including difficulties competing with its siblings for survival and possible rejection by its mother.

[28] Pheromones are a chemical substance produced and released into the environment by an animal, especially a mammal or an insect, affecting the behavior or physiology of others of its species. Pigs have many pheromones including: 1) sexual pheromones (male, female, gilt development), 2) maternal-neonatal pheromones, 3) stress-related pheromones, 4) aggressive and submissive pheromones. Pigs sniff when they encounter a new or interesting odor.

At that point, fatty tissue begins developing just under the skin (**subcutaneous**), measuring three-quarters to over an inch (2-3 cm) thick near the shoulder blades to the rump. This layer seems to protect their vital organs during male-to-male dominance fights.

Pregnant sows build farrowing nests within 24 hours before giving birth to their litters. This structure's primary

Land that has been rooted by hogs can take several years before they return to their original state.

function has been theorized as providing the newborn piglets with protection from inclement weather conditions. The litter size in feral sows reportedly decreases after about the 5th-7th litter or around 4-5 years of age. The oldest known wild sow documented to be still capable of breeding was 14 years of age.

When it's time to give birth, females will leave the herd temporarily to construct a nest. The newborn litter will stay

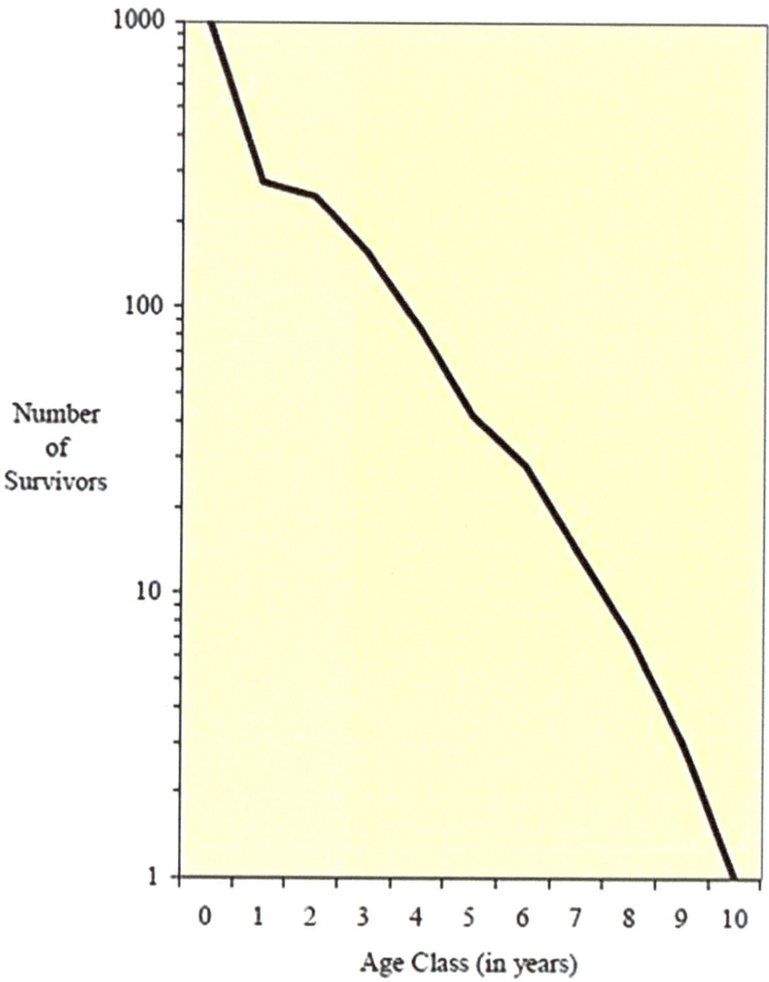

Approximately 50% die before reaching one year of age. In spite of the high fatality rate, wild hogs continue to increase in number and range each year.

at the nest for 4-6 days before rejoining the herd. The birth of the piglets takes place in the nest. The young are typically born with the sow lying on her side but can take place with the sow lying on her belly or standing. A wild boar herd shares responsibility for feeding the litters, which means piglets can suckle from unrelated lactating females within the herd even. The suckling lasts for 3-4 months, and the piglets will reach full maturity at 18 months.

After being born, the piglets almost immediately begin to seek out the teats to start suckling. The piglets do not follow the mother's birth. They will stay within or directly around the farrowing nest for the first 1-2 weeks of life. During that time, the sow will make periodic but infrequent foraging trips away from the

Some success has been shown in trapping wild boars to control populations.

nest. Most of the time, the sow will stay in close physical contact with her litter to keep them warm, as well as near the nest to protect them from potential predators.

Eventually, the family group expands its foraging range gradually further away from the nest site. The sow will continue to lead and protect her litter through weaning and up until they leave the family group. She will defend her piglets at any cost. Reports of bravery exhibited by wild sows defending their young are legendary but possibly exaggerated beyond reality.

Newborn piglets learn to run to their mother's voice as soon as they are up on their feet. A pig's squeal can be as loud as 115 decibels, about as loud as a chainsaw. Pigs communicate constantly.

The maximum lifespan in the wild is 10–14 years, though few specimens survive past 4–5 years. Some boars in captivity have been recorded

to have lived for 20 years.

Miscellaneous

Wild boars are known to display aggressive behavior and are known to kill their predators with their canines, sharpened by constant friction against opposite canine teeth. They may also attack in groups, displaying mobbing behavior. The ferocity of wild boars increases when protecting their young.

Javelinas, and especially the wild hogs, are so adapted for survival they exploit the ecosystem they are in, in such a way as to do nearly irreparable damage. Add to this their

productive ability to **propagate** (produce offspring), and we have one of the fastest-growing, fastest-spreading animals on the planet. Recent studies have shown that the wild hog population is increasing across the United States by as much as 20% yearly!

Areas that have been rooted by *drift* or *driven* by hogs and the soil will not fully recover for many years. Plants, trees, saplings, and vines are damaged or destroyed by swine.

A field rooted by wild boars.

This disruption can occur from roughly rubbing against their bodies, consuming seeds and seedlings, and turning over the soil killing plants and grass and causing the moisture to dry out. The scraping of bark off with their tusks to mark territory often creates an entry point for tree diseases. It is almost needless to say that wild hogs are labeled the *least concern* of species by the International Union for Conservation of Nature's (IUCN) Red List due to their wide range, high numbers, and adaptability to a diversity of habitats.

An introduced and invasive species, wild boars outcompete other animals in the wild. Feral hogs, however, can and should be managed through proper land and wildlife management. While recreational hunting is often a preferred method, it does not effectively control wild pig population growth. However, trapping has been reported as being highly effective in doing so.

Though pork is widely eaten and enjoyed in North America, few people have ever dined on wild pork. Wild boar meat is a leaner and darker red than ordinary pork. Wild boar meat has an intense, sweet, and nutty flavor due to its wild diet of grasses, nuts, and forage. If not on the typical family menu, it could be a useful source to provide food to people with such needs.

Though many wild animals are better left to succeed as they

may, ignoring the wild boar would eventually ruin millions of acres of woodlands. Their outcompeting other animals may benefit them but at the expense of other wildlife, which could find themselves being threatened or worse. **Wild boars and Peccary** are wonders of nature, but they are **disruptive invaders**.

REVIEW

1. What are the two types of feral pigs in North America?

2. What do the terms *indigenous* and *invasive* mean, and how does this relate to wild boars?

3. Using the map, what state has the highest population of wild boars?

4. Where would one most likely find Javelinas?

5. What is a male hog called? Female? Baby hog?

6. What kind of social groups do wild hogs develop?

7. What is a ruminant, and why are hogs nonruminants?

8. List four characteristics of wild hogs.

9. Why do hogs root, and what effect does it have on the soil?

10. Why are wild boars' tusks so sharp and dangerous?

WILD BOAR HOG RUNNING

COLORING PAGE

http://www.supercoloring.com/coloring-pages/running-wild-boar

Name:_________________

Wild Boars & Peccaries: Destructive Invaders

Carefully read the clue provided and complete the crossword puzzle below. Use the Word Bank as needed.

symbiotic   anthropomorphism   diurnal   lactating   Porky   mud   Texas   gestation   glands   rooting

endothermic   behaviors   tusks   squadron   Piccaries

Across

1. Grow at a rate of about one-fourth inch per month.
3. Mother's production of milk.
5. Relationship in which two organisms both benefit from one another.
6. Provides some comfort from insects and heat of summer.
8. To add human-like qualities to an animal or object.
11. An classic pig cartoon character.
12. Scent marking usually involves __________.
13. Period of time when offspring are growing in the uterus.

Down

1. State with the highest population of wild hogs?
2. Animal able to generate their own body heat by metabolizing.
4. Active mostly during the daylight hours.
5. Group of peccaries traveling and living together
7. Wild boars and peccaries seem to have some of the most complex __________.
9. Another name for razorbacks?
10. To dig in the earth and dirt for roots and grubs.

INTERESTING SOURCES TO CONSIDER

Animal Fact Sheet: Collared Peccary or Javelina. Available at: https://www.desertmuseum.org/kids/oz/long-fact-sheets/Javelina.php

Attack of Hogzilla. National Geographic Wild. Available at: https://youtu.be/mGbXHZjdEbw

Celebrating and Exploring The Fascinating Lives Of Pigs! Animal Adventures. Available at: https://youtu.be/DYNSKVyU5Wg

Coping with Feral Hogs. Frequently Asked Questions-Wild Pigs. Available at: https://feralhogs.tamu.edu/frequently-asked-questions/frequently-asked-questions-wild-pigs/

Dealing with feral hogs. Available at: https://youtu.be/xF5wKcYHE3c

Feral Hogs in North Texas - A Growing Urban Issue. Available at: https://youtu.be/nAaYCMfztBk

Feral Pig Research And Management Documentary. Available at: https://youtu.be/4zbw2NysvVo

Giant Wild Boars Documentary.. Available at: https://youtu.be/urU_-UM4n2M

Hog Genius. Awesome Animals. Available at: https://youtu.be/gybZTSfTSZA

Managing Wild Hogs: A Technical Guide. Available at: https://www.aphis.usda.gov/wildlife_damage/feral_swine/pdfs/managing-feral-pigs.pdf

MonsterQuest: 1,000 Pound Wild Boar Gets Aggressive (S2, E1). Full Episode. Available at: https://youtu.be/KyCUYGbpo6A

Mysterious Giant Forest Hog: Rare Footage. National Geographic Wild. Available at: https://youtu.be/3LEt-0iOyek

Vicious Wild Boar Hog. Available at: https://youtu.be/pzpVfQn_oD0

War on hogs: Fight against 500k feral pigs in Louisiana. Available at: https://youtu.be/09KcndZGlQU

Wild Hogs Are Taking Over Florida! Episode 1 - It's A Wild Life. Available at: https://youtu.be/LBCTCUz284o

Wild pigs are invading Canadian provinces and it's kind of a big deal. Your Morning. Available at: https://youtu.be/HuAoQR0Yeqw

Wild Pigs: Biology, Damage, Control Techniques, and Management. Available at: https://sti.srs.gov/fulltext/SRNL-RP-2009-00869.pdf

ABOUT THE AUTHOR

Richard NeSmith is a native of Florida, USA. He grew up wading through the swamps of central Florida with his two younger brothers during the pre-Disney era, and unknowingly, falling in love with biology, wildlife, and nature. He has lived in seven American states, twice in Australia, and once in Mexico City. He holds eight university degrees and has taught for 14 years in secondary schools, here and abroad, and another 13 years as a professor in several American universities. His service includes professor of science education, Dean of Education, Campus Dean, as well as an online instructor. His passion for learning (and *how we learn*) did not develop until *after* graduating from high school. His only explanation for this is that *having a goal made all the difference in the world*. He enjoys reading, hiking, nature photography, golf, tennis, and R.V. camping.

http://richardnesmith.obior.cc

Applied Principles of Education & Learning presents

APE-Learning

AMAZON AUTHOR's PAGE:

https://www.amazon.com/author/richardnesmith

Educational, wildlife, and naturalist books
Dr. Richard NeSmith.

Issue 1
Raccoons:
Friendly Bandits
Dr. Richard NeSmith

Issue 2
Sandhill Cranes
&
Pileated Woodpeckers
Flaming Redheads
Dr. Richard NeSmith

Issue 3
American
Alligators
&
Crocodiles
Dr. Richard NeSmith

Issue 4
Bobcats:
Ghostly Elusive
Dr. Richard NeSmith

Issue 5
Foxes:
Sneaky Rascals
Dr. Richard NeSmith

Issue 6
Armadillo:
Little Armored One
Dr. Richard NeSmith

Issue 7
Squirrels:
Bushy Tail Scampers
Dr. Richard NeSmith

Issue 8
River Otters:
Aquatic Clowns!
Dr. Richard NeSmith

Issue 9
Beavers:
Nature's Engineers !
Dr. Richard NeSmith

Issue 10
Black Bears
Titans of the Forest
Dr. Richard NeSmith

Issue 11
Freshwater
Turtles
Dr. Richard NeSmith

Issue 12
FUNGI, LICHENS
& MUSHROOMS
Dr. Richard NeSmith

Paperbacks: http://amazon.com/author/richardnesmith

e-books: https://bit.ly/3iuCgB3

---

[i] **Special thanks to the following who kindly provided permission to use their photographs.**

From Pixabay: PatternPictures, Calvin Tatum, Russ Critendon, Eveline de Bruin, sandid, Ben Kerckx, and Vinson Tan. Special thanks and mention to Rene Rauschenberger for the photograph that made a wonderful book cover.

Finally, *special thanks* to likeminded friends who love wildlife and who willingly shared their wonderful photos, and many of whom have become my friends: **Dr. Laurie Aleixo**, **Bonnie Williams Anderson Tom Dotson**, **Cindy Frasier**, **Gail Halm**, and **Dan Rieck.**

Special thanks to the United States Department of Agriculture who have, along with several of their Cooperative Extensions, provided a great deal of information on wild hogs in the United States.

Thank you everyone.